日常会話編

絵で おぼえる 英会話

REAL Talking in the Office by Ellie Oh
© Ellie Oh, 2012

Originally published by Woongjin Think Big Co., Ltd. in Korea.
All rights reserved.
Japanese copyright © 2023 by Bunkyosha Co., Ltd.,
Japanese translation rights arranged with Woongjin Think Big Co., Ltd. through Danny Hong Agency

「アレ、英語でどう言うんだっけ…」におさらば！

 「英語だけ」なのにわかる！ だから身につく！

「留学前に何をしたらいいのかわからない」「海外に行ってみたいけど不安だなあ」と思ったら、**この1冊で海外生活を「予習」して**みましょう！

　本書は2011年に韓国で発売され、発売後6ヶ月以上にわたりランキング1位を独占したロング・ベストセラー。その人気の秘密は、**本番さながらのシチュエーションを体験することで自然と表現が身につく「Real Talking」メソッド。**難しい問題や解説は一切ナシ！ ストーリーを楽しむだけ！ 1人でも手軽に取り組めて、覚えたフレーズも忘れません。

 楽しいから続く、充実の全22シチュエーション！

　本書には**日常生活のさまざまなシチュ**エーションを収録。海外にいる気分で繰り返し、聞いて、話して、書いて、Annaとの冒険を楽しんでください。**英語力と自信を身につけて、あなたの海外生活をスタートさせましょう！**

5つの特長

1 Fun!
楽しい

まるでその場にいるかのよう! Real Talking では実際の場面を体感できるから、楽しくマンガを読むだけでフレーズがスラスラ覚えられます。主人公Annaと一緒に、さあ出かけましょう!

2 Useful!
役に立つ

今日から使える簡単フレーズが盛り沢山！ そのほか海外Q&Aや関連単語も併せて覚えられるから、実生活で生きてくる本当の英語力が身につきます！

3 Easy!
簡単

飽き性の人も心配無用！ 全てのセリフをアメリカ人ナレーターが読み上げた付属音声や、14日間完成のおすすめ学習スケジュールがついているから、手軽なのに1人でもしっかり成果が出ます！

4 Only English!
本格的

本文は英語だけ！ でも心配はいりません。初めて言葉を覚える子どものように、ストーリーを楽しむうちに自然と英語を英語のまま理解できるようになります。シンプルな日常会話とはいえ、英語を英語で覚えることは真の英語力向上への最短ルートです。

5 Repeat!
忘れない

用途別に活用できる4種の付属音声のほか、スペリングチェックにも使えるミニテスト、ディクテーション編もついているから、何度もリピート学習できてフレーズを忘れる心配はありません。

CONTENTS

本 編

巻末付録

付属音声について

各種音声のくわしい活用方法は「おすすめ学習スケジュール&本書の使い方」(8・9ページ)をご覧ください。

Real リアル

実際の英会話に近いスピードでセリフを読み上げた音声です。BGMや効果音入りなので、まるでその場にいるかのような感覚で学ぶことができます。はじめは聞き取れなくても大丈夫。わからないところは何度も聞き、だんだんと速さに慣れていきましょう。

Shadowing シャドーイング

「リアル」よりもゆっくり、一語一語をはっきりと読み上げた文章です。聞き取れない部分を確認したり、リピートして発音を練習したりするのに最適です。

Role Play ロールプレイ

「リアル」から Anna のセリフのみを取り除いた音声です。Annaになりきって登場人物たちと会話してみましょう。

Let's Review レッツレビュー

各スキットにおける重要フレーズの確認クイズの音声です。学習後に活用し、理解度をチェックしましょう。

ダウンロード方法

本書の音声は「ストリーミング再生」と「音声ダウンロード」の2通りでご利用いただけます。

ストリーミング再生

📱 **スマホの場合**
右の QR コードを読み取り、「付属音声ダウンロード&ストリーミング再生」にアクセスしてください。

🖥 **パソコンの場合**
① 下記のURLを入力し、「付属音声ダウンロード&ストリーミング再生」にアクセスしてください。
https://bunkyosha.com/books/9784866516189/article/1

② または、文響社の公式サイトにアクセスし、右上の検索バー(「書籍を検索する」と表示されている枠)に「絵でおぼえる英会話」と打ち込んでください。表示された表紙画像をクリックし、「付属音声ダウンロード&ストリーミング再生」をクリックしてください。
https://bunkyosha.com/

音声ダウンロード

1 上記いずれかの方法で「付属音声ダウンロード&ストリーミング再生」にアクセスしてください。

2 「ダウンロードはこちら」から、「音声ダウンロード」ボタンをクリックします。

3 端末に「絵でおぼえる英会話 日常会話編 .zip」というZIPファイルがダウンロードされます。解凍(展開)すると、中に音声データ(MP3形式)が入っていますので、用途に合わせてご利用ください。

※音声データ(MP3形式)を再生するには、ダウンロードした ZIP ファイルを解凍(展開)する必要があります。

わたしも

感動の声、
続々!

{ **Real Talking** } で

話せるようになりました!

VOICE 01
▶大阪府
さくさん

文字ばかりだとやる気がなくなってしまうけど、
シンプルでイラストもあるこの本なら、
自分にもできると思いました。

VOICE 02
▶兵庫県
Rinさん

シンプルな英語のみで
会話の自然な流れがつかみやすい!

VOICE 03
▶東京都
みきはなさん

フレーズを自然に覚えることができるので、
日常会話編で中級レベル以上のものも
ぜひ出してほしいです!

VOICE 04
▶神奈川県
メクメクさん

日本語の解説がなく、英語のみだったので、
英語で考える力がつくのを感じられた。

※『絵でおぼえる英会話 ビジネス編』に寄せられた読者の皆様の声を掲載しています。

💬 右のQRコードからご感想をお寄せください。

読者アンケートにご回答いただいたお客様には、「Dictation Book」無料
PDFを配布しております。プリントアウトして繰り返しディクテーション練習
するなど、学習にぜひお役立てください(アンケートの最後にアクセス用の
リンクをご案内しています)。

14- day schedule

14日間で誰でもペラペラに!

Real Talking

おすすめ学習スケジュール

14日間完成

Day 1	Day 2	Day 3
START!	12~41 ページ	42~75 ページ
12~140 ページ		

Day 4	Day 5	Day 6	Day 7
76~105 ページ	106~140 ページ	12~75 ページ	76~140 ページ

Day 8	Day 9	Day 10	Day 11
141~167 ページ	168~197 ページ	198~223 ページ	224~254 ページ

Day 12	Day 13	Day 14	
12~75 ページ	76~140 ページ	12~140 ページ	FINISH!

8

本書の使い方

1 想像する -

 まずは通しでストーリーを読んでみましょう。場面ごとに「使ってみたいフレーズ」「知らなかったフレーズ」などを頭に浮かべてみてください。

2 聞く -

音声を聞きながら、最初は心の中で、慣れたら口に出して、セリフをまねてみましょう。1回20分程度なので、1日2回、通勤や通学などのすきま時間を活用するのがおすすめ!

3 話してみる - - - - - - - - - - - - - - - - - - -

音声を聞きながら、ナレーターの抑揚や間の取り方などをまねて声に出します。慣れてきたら本を見ずに挑戦してみましょう。

4 書き取る -

 「Dictation Book」(141ページ以降)を使って、ディクテーション(ページ下部参照)の練習をしてみましょう。まずは Let's Review ①〜④の空欄を使って練習をしてから「Dictation Book」に進むのがおすすめです。リスニングだけでなくスペリングも鍛えられます。

5 会話する -

 友人や家族と役割を分担して話してみましょう。お互いのスピーキング力向上につながります。1人の場合は、音声を活用して実際の会話のつもりで話します。自分の声を録音して、発音をチェックするのも効果的。

英語力がさらにアップ!
ディクテーションとは?

 「ディクテーション」とは、音声を聞いて行う書き取り練習のこと。リスニングにもスペリングの強化にも効果的です。まず音声を聞き、そのまま書き取ります。1回で全て書き取れなければ、30秒程度で区切り、繰り返し聞いて完成させます。最後までわからない部分は、その理由がリスニング(聞き取れなかった)なのか、スペリング(綴りがわからなかった)なのかを確認しましょう。同じ教材で繰り返し行うのがおすすめです。

You can choose the size.
1oz = 30ml = 30g

13

Add toppings
according to your taste.

18

What You Can Do in an Electronics Store

look at and test merchandise

ask for after-sales service

AFTER-SALES SERVICE

purchase accessories

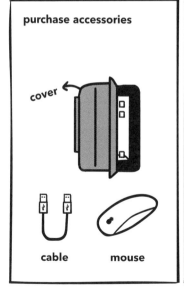

cover

cable   mouse

charge your cell phone and use the Wi-Fi for free

Excuse me.
I'm looking for
a correction tape
and a glue stick.

You can find them
in the office
supplies section.

Office Supplies

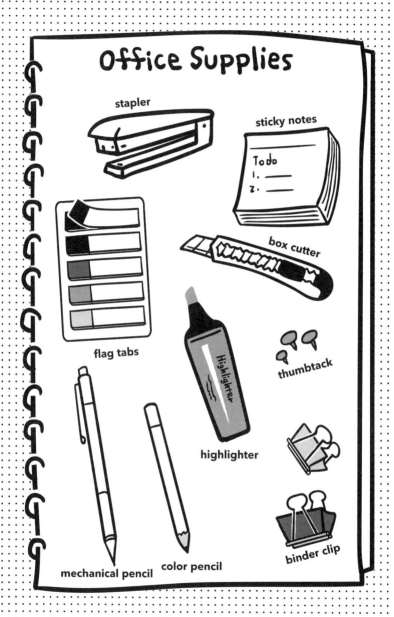

Office Supplies

stapler

sticky notes

To Do
1. ___
2. ___

flag tabs

box cutter

highlighter

thumbtack

binder clip

mechanical pencil

color pencil

When Ordering a Pizza

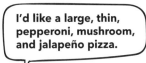

I'd like a large, thin, pepperoni, mushroom, and jalapeño pizza.

I'd like a half-cheese, half-pepperoni pizza.

Anything else?

No, that will be all.

I have a free drink coupon.

33

Did you find everything alright?

Yup.

Do you have a library card?

No. Can I get one?

Sure.

We need your ID and a letter that shows your address.

If You Want to Reserve Books...

They send you a notice
when the book is ready.

Useful Tips for Using the Library

If returning books
when the library is closed,
put them into the drop box.

You have to pay a fine for
a damaged or late book.

Same County

You can use your
library card at
any public library
in the county where you live.

They sometimes offer
free classes.

A How much?

B Here you are.

C When will you get some in?

D Excuse me. I'm looking for a correction tape and a glue stick.

E How would you like to pay?

F It's so nice of you.

G It's for delivery.

H Yes, that's right. How long will it take?

I No. Can I get one?

J Please fill this out.

Maybe I should get a cell phone.

Welcome to Horizon. How can I help you?

I want to buy a prepaid phone.

Please take a look.

	$3/day	$1/day
Talk	Unlimited	10 minutes
Text	Unlimited	Unlimited
Data	Unlimited	–

44

Calling in the U.S.

1. There are 3 major mobile phone companies in the U.S.: Verizon, AT&T, and T-Mobile.

---

2. Unless you have an unlimited plan, there is a fee for all incoming and outgoing calls, text messages and data use.

---

3. Your phone number consists of a country code, area code, and the phone number.

1 - 213 - 369 - 0000

country code   area code   phone number

A savings account is
for saving money.

A checking account is
for both deposits
and withdrawals.

With a debit card,
the money is taken from
your bank account right
away.

With a credit card,
you get a monthly bill
from the card company.

American Banking Information

In the U.S., you don't use a passbook to access your account.

You receive a bank statement every month via mail or email.

You may pay your bills with personal checks.

53

You may need to ask a store employee for assistance to use the fitting room.

Leave the items that you don't want in the fitting room.

You may try on underwear.

No price is shown on the gift receipt.

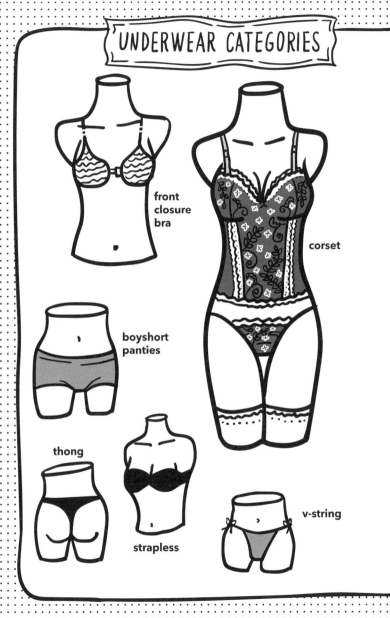

UNDERWEAR CATEGORIES

front closure bra

corset

boyshort panties

thong

strapless

v-string

babydoll

push-up
bra

boxers

garter

briefs

Hello.
How may I help you?

I'd like to have these pants and this dress dry-cleaned.

No problem.

Bring your claim ticket when you return to pick up your items.

Would You Like Anything Else?

66

Now Let's Start Warming Up!

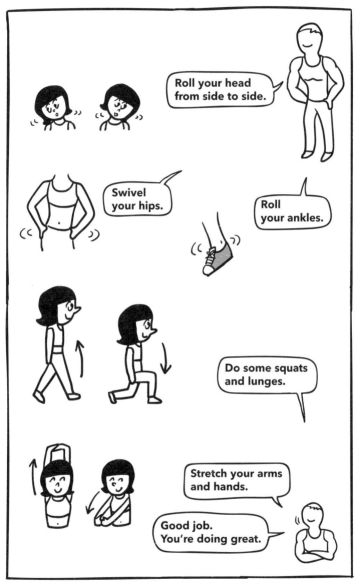

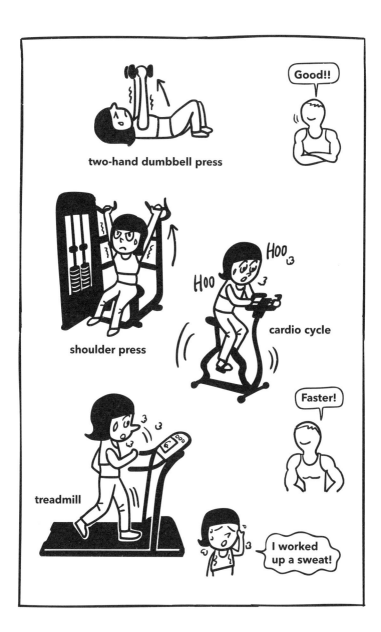

How to Use a Coin Laundry

Absolutely "Not" Responsible for LOST or STOLEN Items.

1. Put your clothes in a washer.

2. Put detergent into the washer.

3. Select the appropriate cycle.

4. Insert money.

5. Wait. It takes about 40 minutes.

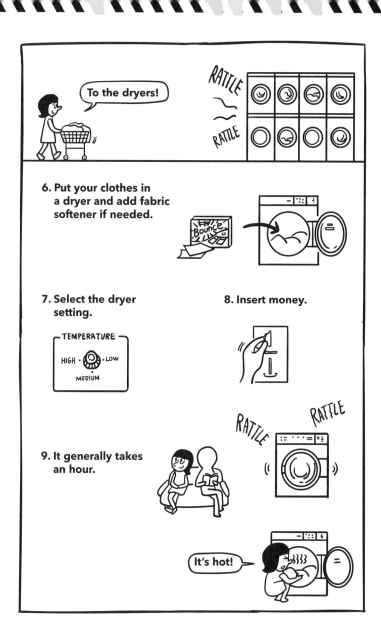

To the dryers!

RATTLE
RATTLE

6. Put your clothes in a dryer and add fabric softener if needed.

Bounce

7. Select the dryer setting.

TEMPERATURE
HIGH · LOW
MEDIUM

8. Insert money.

9. It generally takes an hour.

RATTLE   RATTLE

It's hot!

A Can you recommend one?
B Right here!
C I'd like to open a new account.
D Excuse me. Could you take my measurements?
E Can I try this on?
F This is a gift. Can I have it gift-wrapped?
G Ready to order?
H I'd like to have these pants and this dress dry-cleaned.
I How much is the annual fee?
J When are you open?

How to Use a Self-Service Gas Station

1. Slide your card quickly.

2. Choose either debit or credit.

3. Enter your PIN or zip code.

4. Remove the nozzle from the pump.

5. Select a fuel grade.

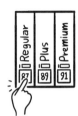

6. Put the nozzle in the tank.

7. When finished, your receipt will be printed.

Off we go!

80

Do you want a shampoo?

Yes, please.

You should tip for the shampoo separately.

How's the water temperature?

It's a bit cold.

All done here.

Isn't it too tight around your neck?

Fine.

Hair Vocabulary

part

bangs

sideburns

What you can have done at a hair salon

hair coloring

hair straightening

thinning out thick hair

hair wave

perm

hair treatment

86

You can put the vegetables into plastic bags.

The cashier will ring them up when you check out.

Oh, I need some meatballs and tomato paste as well.

Your total is $78.99.

Debit, please.

You want cash back?

No, thanks.

What's Cash Back?

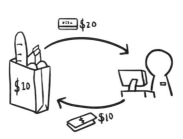

1. For example,
   your total is $10,
   and you have no cash.

2. Pay $20
   with your debit card.

3. Get $10 back in cash
   at the cash register.

Grocery Store

naturals & organics

fresh produce

meat

delicatessen

bakery

snacks

frozen

packaged dinners

dairy

canned goods

beverages

diapers

beauty

greeting cards & floral

Making Spaghetti and Meatballs

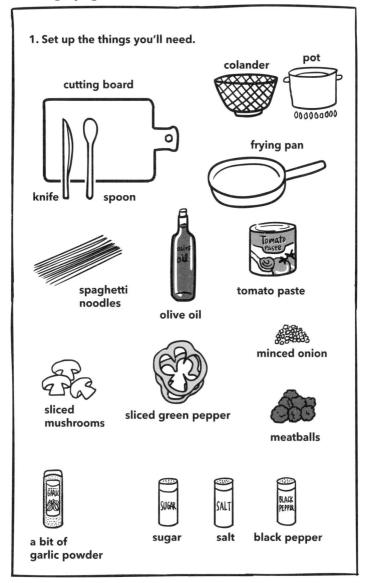

1. Set up the things you'll need.

cutting board

colander

pot

frying pan

knife   spoon

spaghetti noodles

olive oil

tomato paste

sliced mushrooms

sliced green pepper

minced onion

meatballs

a bit of garlic powder

sugar

salt

black pepper

2. Boil some water.

 3. Brown the meatballs over medium heat.

 4. Pour the tomato paste into the pan.

 5. Simmer it at a low heat.

 6. Add the dry noodles when the water is boiling.

 7. Stir occasionally for about 10 minutes.

 8. Drain the water.

 9. Serve the sauce over the spaghetti.

 yummy

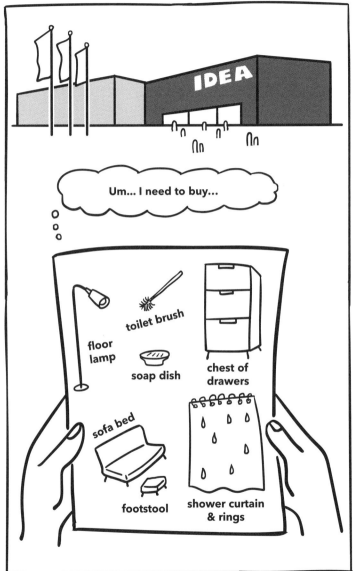

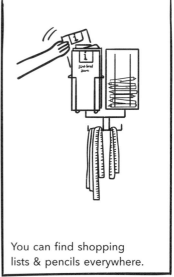

You can find shopping lists & pencils everywhere.

Oh, it's a sofa bed!

Excuse me. I'd like to get the sofa bed.

Hold on. I'll give you a sales order.

Take this to the cashier when you check out.

After that, you can pick it up.

Thanks.

The delivery desk is located just past the checkout counters.

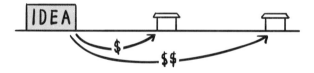

The delivery fee depends on the delivery distance.

Tip the delivery person.

A Where are you headed?
B Can I give you a ride?
C Hello. Do you have an appointment?
D What do you have in mind?
E Please take off a little more here.
F Which one should I get?
G I'll go with the 2% reduced fat.
H Yes! This is exactly what I'm looking for.
I Excuse me. I'd like to get the sofa bed.
J You take care.

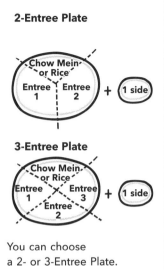

Pick up your chopsticks, straws, and napkins at the register.

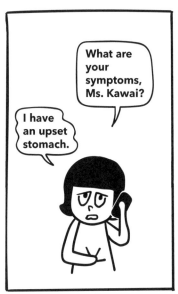

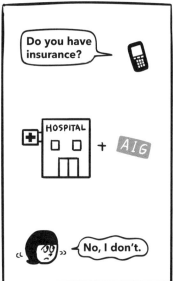

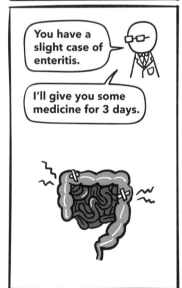

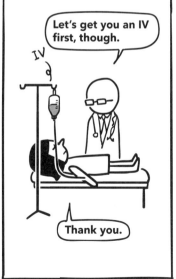

116

I'll try this canned soup.

I'm Anna Kawai. I'm back for my medication.

Um... Oh, here it is. $10.

Please add this, too.

OK.

A studio is a small apartment with one room.

119

Utilities include water, gas, and electricity.

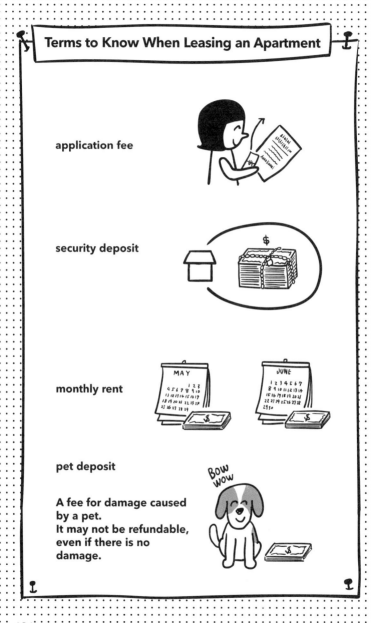

Terms to Know When Leasing an Apartment

application fee

security deposit

monthly rent

MAY

JUNE

pet deposit

A fee for damage caused
by a pet.
It may not be refundable,
even if there is no
damage.

BOW
WOW

Types of Housing in the U.S.

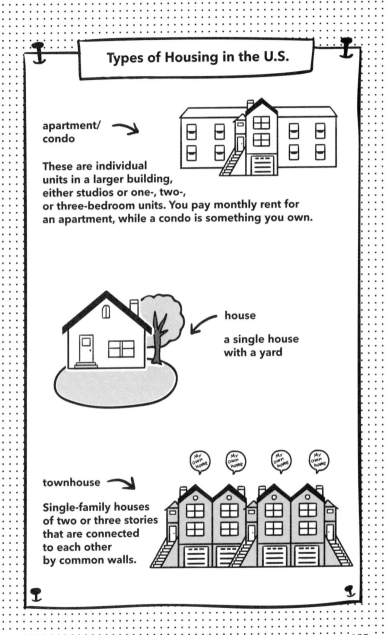

apartment/ condo

These are individual units in a larger building, either studios or one-, two-, or three-bedroom units. You pay monthly rent for an apartment, while a condo is something you own.

house

a single house with a yard

townhouse

Single-family houses of two or three stories that are connected to each other by common walls.

Oh, they have an in-town special?

I'm here to rent a moving truck.

May I see your driver's license?

Sure.

Rental Truck

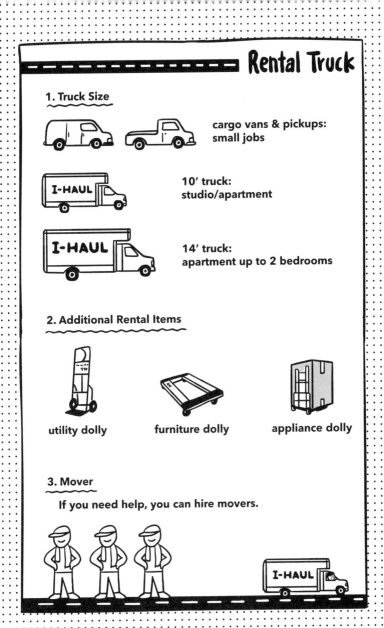

1. Truck Size

cargo vans & pickups:
small jobs

I-HAUL

10' truck:
studio/apartment

I-HAUL

14' truck:
apartment up to 2 bedrooms

2. Additional Rental Items

utility dolly

furniture dolly

appliance dolly

3. Mover

If you need help, you can hire movers.

I-HAUL

After Moving in...

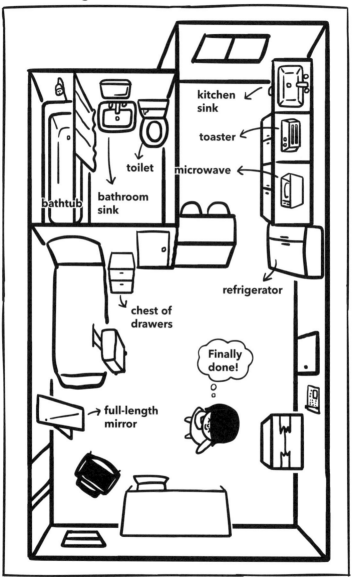

This is the original Starlucks!

Wow, there are a lot of people in line.

oh!!

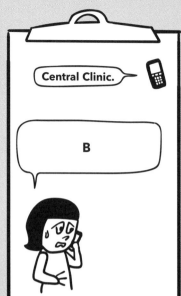

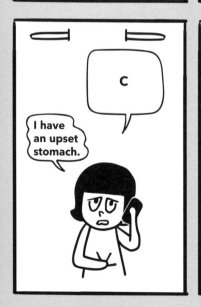

A For here or to go?

B Hello. This is Anna Kawai. I'm calling to make an appointment.

C What are your symptoms, Ms. Kawai?

D What brings you here today?

E Hello. May I have your prescription?

F Is a six-month lease possible?

G OK. Is it furnished?

H Sure. I'll be there by four.

I Hmm... I just have a studio apartment. What do you recommend?

J Can I have a grande latte?

Dictation Book

ディクテーション編

= 30ml =

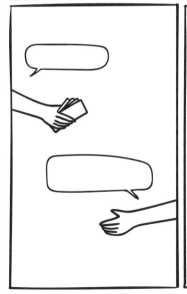

What You Can Do in an Electronics Store

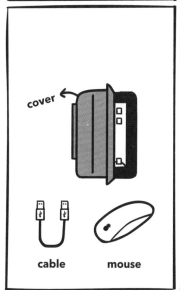

Office Supplies

150

Office Supplies

154

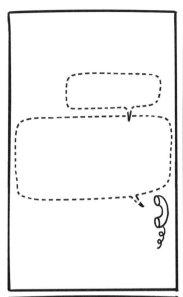

Thirty minutes later...

When Ordering a Pizza

If You Want to Reserve Books...

Useful Tips for Using the Library

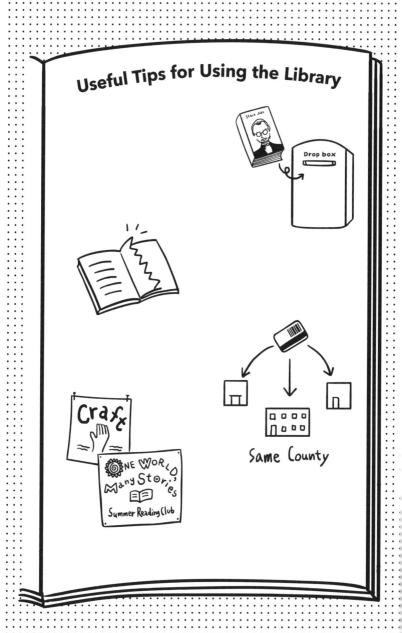

	$3/day	$1/day
Talk	Unlimited	10 minutes
Text	Unlimited	Unlimited
Data	Unlimited	–

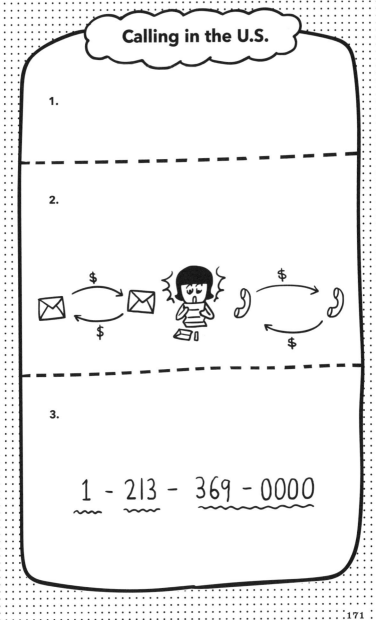

Calling in the U.S.

1.

2.

3.

1 - 213 - 369 - 0000

172

After a while...

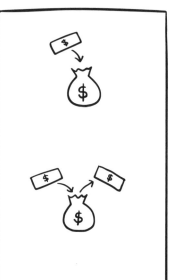

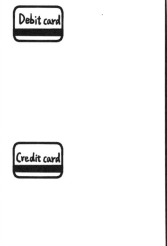

175

American Banking Information

189

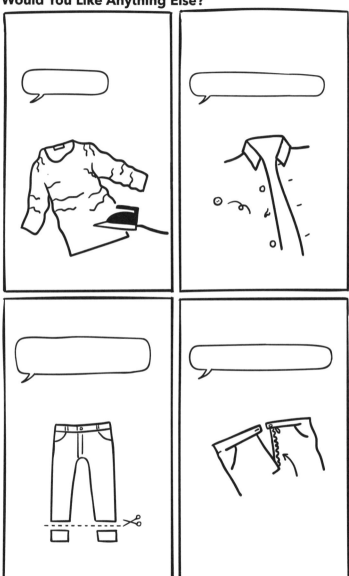

Now Let's Start Warming Up!

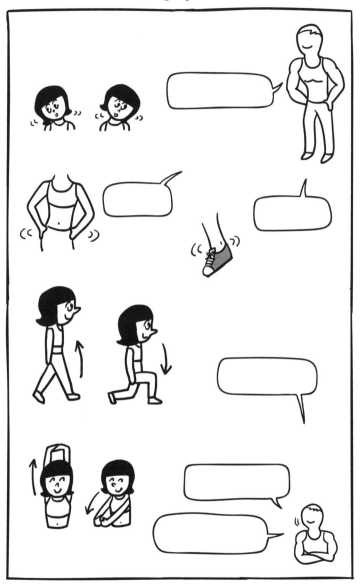

How to Use a Coin Laundry

Absolutely "Not" Responsible for LOST or STOLEN Items.

1.

2.

3.

START HOT WARM COLD

4.

5.

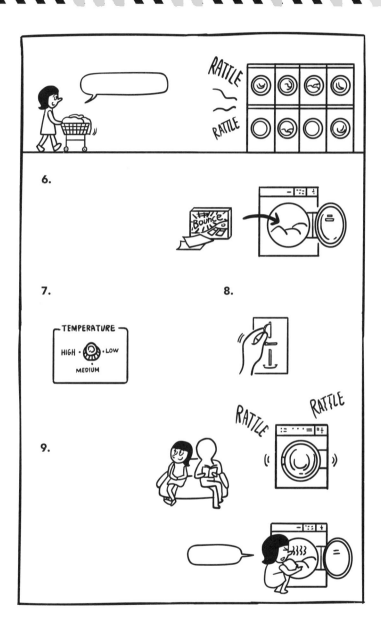

6.

7.

8.

9.

Beep
Beep

How to Use a Self-Service Gas Station

1.

2.

3.

4.

5.

6.

7.

SNIP
SNIP

SNIP
SNIP

Hair Vocabulary

What you can have done at a hair salon

=

208

What's Cash Back?

1.

2.

3.

Making Spaghetti and Meatballs

1.

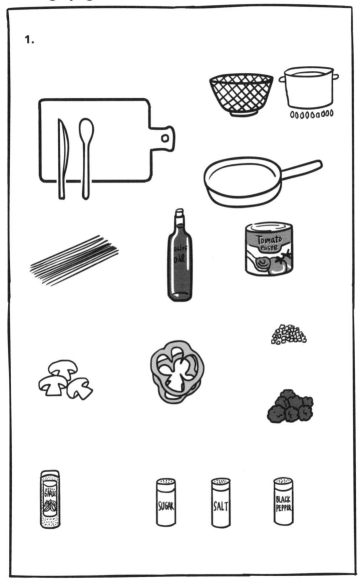

2.

3.

4.

5.

6.

7.

8.

9.

yummy

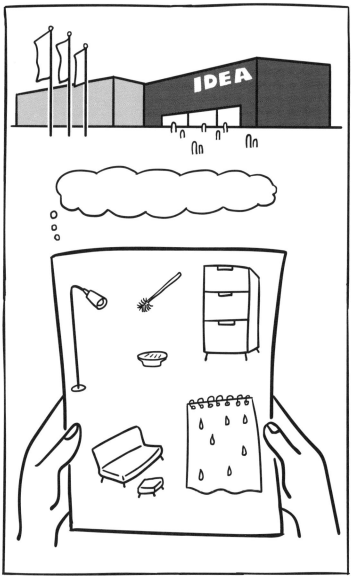

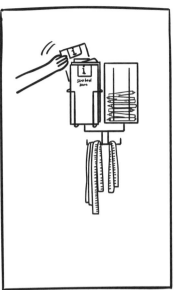

SELF-SERVE
FURNITURE
AREA

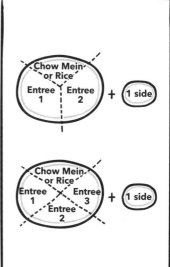

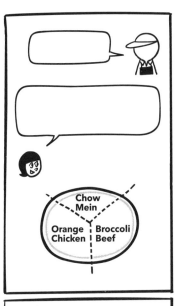

After a few hours...

A bit later...

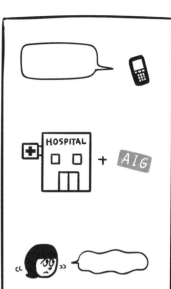

The next day...

A few minutes later...

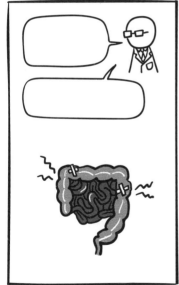
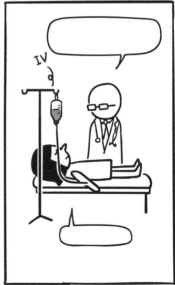

233

234

239

240

The next day...

RING
RING

Terms to Know When Leasing an Apartment

Types of Housing in the U.S.

244

245

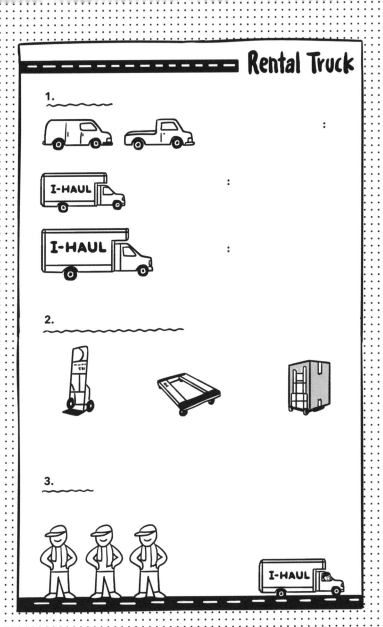

Rental Truck

1. ___

:

:

:

2. ___

3. ___

251

著者

エリー・オー
Ellie Oh

アメリカの現地シニアデザイナー、フィリピンの国際学校
ディレクター、韓国の英語講師および著者として多様な経歴
をもつ。日常のさまざまなシーンに即したリアルな英語と異
文化理解に関心が深い。幼稚園児から社会人、シニアに至る
まで、幅広い年齢層の生徒に教えた経験をもとに「生きた英
語」を伝えるための活動を行っている。自身がアメリカの企
業に勤めたときの苦労や発見をもとに、本書を執筆した。

絵でおぼえる英会話　日常会話編

2023 年 4 月 11 日　第 1 刷発行

著　　　者	エリー・オー
編　　　者	ターシャ・キム／アンナ・ヤン
デザイン	小寺練
イラスト	サンダースタジオ
翻訳協力	三嶋圭子
校　　正	田中国光
DTP制作	川瀬結芽
英文校閲	リサ・ウィルカット
音声録音・編集	ELEC（一般財団法人 英語教育協議会）
編　　集	一柳沙織
発 行 人	山本周嗣
発 行 所	株式会社文響社
	〒105-0001
	東京都港区虎ノ門 2-2-5　共同通信会館 9F
	ホームページ　https://bunkyosha.com
	お問い合わせ　info@bunkyosha.com
印刷・製本	中央精版印刷株式会社

読者アンケート
実施中！
くわしくは本書の
7ページをチェック！